D0268759

Terry:

May all your Transitions

Turn out to be Journeys of Joy.

John Nedowmer ☺

D0268763

TRANSITIONS

A Journey of Joy

Facing Transitions Without Fear

JOHN DODSWORTH

TRANSITIONS
A Journey of Joy

Copyright 2012 by John Dodsworth

All rights reserved. No Portion of this Book may be reproduced in any form without written permission of the author except as provided by USA copyright law.

Unless otherwise indicated, all Scriptural quotations are taken from the Holy Bible, New International Version, Copyright 1973, 1978, 1984 by the International Bible Society. Used by permission of Zondervan Publishing House. All rights reserved.

ISBN 13: 978–1475052916

Printed in the United States of America

WITH A JOYFUL AND THANKFUL HEART
I DEDICATE THIS BOOK TO:

Jerry Jones
*Thanks Bro, for having
an open and sharing heart
on July 10, 1987*

Dr. Lamont Jacobs
*Thanks Jake, for truly having
the heart of a servant*

IN LOVING MEMORY OF THOMAS F. HARLOW
1938 - 2011

WITH SPECIAL THANKS

To my Wife, Letty
*Thank you for patiently listening to me all
through the composition of this book.*

and

To Gail Webster and Marti Buttrill
*Thank you for the love that you put into
this book through your editing and spiritual
insights, and for being my sounding boards.*

and

To Diana Stroh and Monica Scalf
*Thank you for guiding me into the
publishing world.*

and

To my Business Partner, Jason Crank
*Thanks for the encouragement and for
taking over the Agency workload so that
I could complete this manuscript.*

and

To Debbie Christy McCurry
Thanks for being my E-F-G

and

To Linda and Sam

TRANSITIONS:
A JOURNEY OF JOY

Introduction

Why this Book?

I didn't realize it at the time, but it started over 15 years ago when I began to journal each day during my quiet time with the Lord. During those morning quiet times, I began to record the thoughts that came to me as I read and meditated in the Scriptures.

But before going any further into my journaling journey, it may be helpful to know what motivated me to step onto that path in the first place.

Part I, "Transitions," deals with the background for my journey. It was during this time that I was blessed to discover just how real God's Word was in helping me to deal with the emotional burdens of a difficult period of transition. For the first time in my life, God's Word became alive to me. I leaned upon it and experienced how the Lord used it to guide and empower me to cope with my personal struggles. If you are one of those folks who is currently involved in a transition in your life, perhaps you might identify with the doubts and fears that were my companions during those years. Those doubts and fears led me to probe deeper into God's Word on a daily basis. The thoughts that were written down in my journal during those morning quiet times became the meditations that are shared in Part III.

Despite encouragement from close friends, I had always dismissed thoughts of publishing any of this material, until it was suggested to me, "If you feel that God has so richly blessed you through these morning meditations, then why would he not use them to bless others as well?" That made sense, so here we are!

An appropriate title for this book could very well be, "The Meditations of a Sinful Man." The experiences and meditations that I share are evidence of how God's grace can work through someone like me. I am a working guy. Sometimes my cash flow gets real clogged up. At times my emotions "fly off the handle." At times, what I am either saying or doing could cause others to look at me and wonder if I actually *am* a Christian man.

So, I have humbly (hopefully!) embarked on a course of sharing my experience during a major transition in my life and the resulting meditations that followed. I have tried to be sensitive to God's leading in this endeavor, as only he knows who the folks are who might benefit from reading through them. Perhaps somewhere along the line, someone going through an unexpected transition in their life might be able to identify with a thought or a meditation that is shared here in a way that brings encouragement. If that should be the case, we can thank the Lord for it. If you are one of those folks, I sincerely hope that this experience will bring even greater joy to you in your walk with him than it has given to me.

John Dodsworth
January 20, 2012

Table of Contents

PART I
TRANSITIONS
The Background for the Journaling Journey

PART II
THE JOURNALING JOURNEY

PART III
SHARING THE MEDITATIONS
A Journey of Joy

PART 1V
TRANSITIONS REVISITED

TRANSITIONS

PART I

The Background For
The Journaling Journey

TRANSITIONS
Transitions

We are all born with hopes and dreams, even though we may not realize it. I believe that these are among the mediums by which God makes known to us the purpose and plan that he has for our lives.

A lot is said about "knowing God's plan for one's life." How many times have you heard someone say, or even said to yourself, "I wish I knew what God's plan was for my life!"

My personal view of this idea centers around two thoughts. One is that in order for any of us to know what God's plan is for our life, we have to communicate with him. Think about it! How can any of us know of someone's plan for what we are supposed to do with any situation, be it our parents, our employers, whoever, unless we communicate with them, unless we listen to them? Sounds almost too mundane, doesn't it?

And yet, how often do we make the time to spend with our Heavenly Father, quietly listening to what he is saying to us, as opposed to our doing all of the talking?

Secondly, I have always believed that part of knowing God's plan for our lives is simply in recognizing that we have a strong desire to do a particular thing, to pursue a particular path. Does it make sense that a loving God, who loved us so much that he sent his only Son to die for us, would have a plan for our lives that involved something that we absolutely hated to do? Really!! Does that make sense? It doesn't to me!

If I have a desire to pursue a certain occupational career path, and it is an honest and ethical pursuit, then I can honestly believe that desire was God-given. That is the starting point for my life's journey in compliance with God's plan for my life. For many folks, this could involve many different careers, but the same conditions would apply. Whether it is one career or several, following God's plan involves doing something that we really want to do.

These thoughts provide the background for how I arrived at the career that I now know that God wanted me to pursue as part of his plan for my life.

Since my early teens, I had always known that I wanted to be an Independent Insurance Agent. That's right, an Independent Insurance Agent. Now, really, John, how many folks grow up with a burning desire for that career? Doesn't sound very glamorous or exciting, does it? Certainly, being a physician, a college professor, a minister of the gospel, a law enforcement officer, a fire fighter or any number of other occupations would be more glamorous.

But this endeavor was appealing to me because it offered the opportunity to work in a field that, while growing up, I had become familiar with and had come to really like. My dad had been a life insurance agent with the Prudential Insurance Company, and it just seemed to be osmosis that his enthusiasm for his work was caught by his son as he was growing up.

Even more appealing was that in being an independent agent I would have the opportunity to operate my own agency. I did not want to work for a big company. I wanted to "fly my own plane." This desire was so deeply ingrained in me that I could not escape it. Over the years I tried to put it aside, but it would never go away. That desire remains my passion to this day.

I share all of this to provide a backdrop for the motivation for the career change that I made in 1987 and for all of the fears, apprehensions and victories that grew out of that motivation.

It was during the early years of this transition into my own business, when I began to see for the very first time just how alive God's Word could be in my everyday life. During that time my morning scripture meditations provided the platform for my journaling.

On the timeline of history's horizon, it seems that we are now in a period of time that is characterized by career changes for many people. In fact, this period may well involve more folks going through "transitions" in their lives than any other time in our recent history.

So, my friend, if you are facing a period of transition in your own life, if you have come to one of those forks in the road that you never thought you would ever come to, if you are faced with challenges that you never dreamed you would encounter, then perhaps some of what is shared from this book will relate to where you are, and will provide some measure of encouragement.

What joy that would bring to my heart!

TRANSITIONS
The Tip of the Sword

"Take the helmet of salvation and the sword of the Spirit, which is the Word of God"
Ephesians 6:17

The dream of having my own insurance agency had been a part of my career mindset since my teenage years. It would not go away. It was as deeply imbedded in me as the blood in my veins. It seemed to always be at the back of mind during every business transaction. It seemed to be especially strong one evening on the drive home from a night-time client visit. Wondering about it always centered on the "how?" How would I ever be able to make it come about? How could it ever happen? Many were the times when I asked myself, "Is this just some kind of crazy dream?"

This was no reflection on the family that I worked for during those earlier years in the insurance business. They were kind and generous people. I have said many times that I looked forward to going to work 99% of the time during those years from 1964 to 1987. Perhaps this casts the best reflection on that family. Of course, this contributed to my confusion about ever leaving that position and starting over again. Many were the times when I reminded myself of the good things about being with those folks. Why then would I ever even consider leaving? At times the back and forth of this nearly drove me crazy.

But a God-given dream will not die. It is not supposed to be squelched. Even though I became more convinced over the course of time that this was a God-given dream, even then those thoughts were all too-often clouded over by confusion.

One summer morning in 1985, over breakfast at a Friendly's restaurant, something happened. The impact of that event was so strong that I can almost feel it to this day. I was meditating in the Psalms when the impact of these words of Psalm 40:1-4 flooded over me as if they were being read by an angel standing by my side:

> *I waited patiently for the L*ORD*;*
> *he turned to me and heard my cry.*
> *He lifted me out of the slimy pit,*
> *out of the mud and mire;*
> *he set my feet on a rock*
> *and gave me a firm place to stand.*
> *He put a new song in my mouth,*
> *a hymn of praise to our God.*
> *Many will see and fear*
> *and put their trust in the L*ORD*.*
> *Blessed is the man*
> *who makes the L*ORD *his trust*

At that moment, I knew! I knew for certain that my dream would become a reality. I think when I left the restaurant that morning my feet were on the ground, but I'm not certain of that – because my spirit had me walking on a cloud.

In the midst of that experience I found myself asking the obvious question, "How? How was it going to happen?" But the amazing thing was at that moment the "how" didn't matter. It really didn't! Knowing that it was going to happen was enough. Somehow, part of that "knowing" was the assurance that the "how" of it all would come along eventually. How great it was that the "knowing" was so strong that the "how" didn't matter. I was so excited that I could hardly contain myself!

The Holy Spirit used those first four verses of Psalm 40 to speak to me, to reassure me that my dream was going to become a reality. The tip of the Sword of God's Spirit touched the inside of my heart in a way that only the Lord can do.

And you know what? Sure enough, over the months that followed the "how" of it all did come along one step at a time.

One step of faith at a time! Oh, how many, many times I have said to myself since then, "Why do you continue to run ahead of the Lord when he has shown you so vividly what it means to trust him one step at a time?"

TRANSITIONS
The Mud and the Mire

"Take the helmet of salvation and the sword of the Spirit, which is the Word of God"
Ephesians 6:17

"He lifted me out of the slimy pit,
out of the mud and mire;
he set my feet on a rock
and gave me a firm place to stand."
Psalm 40:2

Despite the impact of that moment on that morning in Friendly's in 1985, over the succeeding months I was still plagued by recurring doubts and fears. I am reluctant to admit to my lack of faith during that period, especially after the Lord had given me such a vivid vision about the fulfillment of my dream. But the questions still persisted.

Back and forth. Should I? Or shouldn't I? Why does this wish tug so strongly at my heart?

Why give up the certainty of:

- a good salary, without the pressures of a pure commission income

- a company car

- a good working environment

- a good client base developed over 23 years

- good opportunities to travel

- one of the top insurance companies in the business to work with

- an agency with an excellent reputation in the community

...for a venture that will have:

- no immediate income and that may never have the income that I have now
- no established client base
- no company car, which means we would have car payments for a replacement vehicle
- having to learn to work with new insurance companies whose products and procedures are totally unfamiliar to me
- very few, if any, opportunities for travel
- having to start from scratch to build a totally new client base

Straight on this appeared to be a "no brainer." Why then? Why this tug at my heart to move on, to fly my own plane? Why that nagging ache that just will never go away? At times, it did seem to vanish from my psyche. But then, back it would come, and I'd realize it had never really left me at all.

The mud and mire in the slimy pit of indecision.

These were not external forces. They were internal for they existed in my mind, in my thoughts. The relentless drive of my desire hounded me so much at times that it became the mud and mire which seemed to hold my thoughts in this paralyzing pattern. My slimy pit was the fear in my stomach – for, truthfully, I was scared to death to walk out on the runway and get into my own plane.

What if we failed? What would people think? Would we lose our home and all of our "things?" How would I view myself if we weren't successful? Would I always feel like a failure?

Like the rays of the sun casting a bright, almost blinding reflection off of the blade of the sword of God's word, I remembered these words from Psalm 37:3-7.

> Trust in the LORD and do good;
> dwell in the land and enjoy safe pasture.
> Delight yourself in the LORD,
> and he will give you the desires of your heart.

Commit your way to the LORD;
trust in him and he will do this:
He will make your righteousness shine like the dawn,
the justice of your cause like the noonday sun.

Be still before the LORD and wait patiently for him.

Then I again remembered Psalm 40:1-4 which had provided the vision some months before:

I waited patiently for the LORD;
he turned to me and heard my cry.
He lifted me out of the slimy pit,
out of the mud and mire;
he set my feet on a rock
and gave me a firm place to stand.
He put a new song in my mouth,
a hymn of praise to our God.
Many will see and fear
and put their trust in the LORD.
Blessed is the man
who makes the LORD his trust.

It was a divinely inspired "fit" reaching down to lift me out of the mud and mire of indecision.

TRANSITIONS
Alive or Dead?

We've all seen those posters from the old westerns with a picture of the bad guy followed by the words, "Reward! Wanted Dead or Alive!" The promise of a monetary award is posted underneath his name, the amount determined by how much of a "bad guy" he really is.

Having finally decided to move ahead on faith, with Letty's help I made a short list of steps that had to be taken in order for our new agency to become a reality. The first was determining where would we get the funds on which to live when we had no idea what our commission income would be. Second was finding insurance companies to represent. The third step involved finding the right persons to hire, and the fourth involved locating and equipping an office. Our prayer became, "Lord, if any one of these doors does not open, that will be our mandate to not move any further beyond that point."

Step one was easily solved through a home equity loan on our home. Step two was more formidable than step one. Insurance companies do not normally give contracts to "scratch" agents. This is the term used in the industry for agents who are just starting out, i.e. starting from "scratch". Companies much prefer to be represented by well established agencies.

During this period, I had become blessed to have a very successful agent as my mentor. In one of our meetings, he suggested that the "XYZ" company would be a good fit in our new agency. He already represented them in his agency, and he offered to contact them to get me an appointment.

So, off I went to see them with my business plan in hand. The people I met with were very cordial. As the interview ended, the president of the company graciously walked me out onto their front porch. As I thanked him for the opportunity to visit with them, in a very kind manner he remarked, "John, we don't give contracts to new agents; however, since you are experienced, we will give this some consideration." I vividly remember the feeling of total peace in my heart as I stood there thinking, "If the Lord wants this to happen, he will open this door." With total peace in my heart, I thanked him and told him that I understood their position, and that if they could not do it, I would certainly understand.

At this stage of the game, we did already have one company to represent; however, I knew that we would need a second carrier in order to be competitive in the marketplace. We had previously made contact with another company about this. Their young field agent in our area was kind enough to meet with me at our home. As we sat at our kitchen table and reviewed my business plan, the look of consternation on his face revealed a definite, "What am I doing here?" mindset. He left, and we never heard from him again.

During the weeks that followed my visit to the "XYZ" company I was inwardly hoping that they would say "no" to my request for representation. The reason for that feeling was very simple. It was fear! I was still afraid to leave a comfortable position in my current agency and step out into the unknown on my own. If these folks turned me down, I would have an excuse to proceed no further into this new venture. "Oh, ye of little faith!" After all the Lord had shown me, that barrier of fear was still hanging around.

And then it happened! One Wednesday afternoon when I was home, I picked up the phone, and the voice on the other end said, "John, this is Dennis at "XYZ." I wanted to call and tell you that we are going to take a chance with you and give you a contract to represent us." I thanked him in the most enthusiastic voice I could conjure up.

Letty had been sitting near the phone, so she had heard my conversation with Dennis. When I told her what he had said, she asked a question that will always remain immortalized in my mind, "What are you going to do now?"

As I stood there just staring at her, going through my mind was a recollection of my recent conversation with the president of "XYZ." At that moment, I knew God had opened the door. Now, would fear have the last word or would God have the last word? My reply to her remains indelibly etched in the depths of my soul: "It is obvious, Honey, that God has opened this door. If we don't move ahead, I will be spiritually dead for the rest of my life. I don't care if we lose everything, I can't bear the thought of that happening. I just can't."

Fortunately, at that moment, God's grace enabled me to see that if I didn't move ahead on faith, I would become an empty shell of a man. The poster that the Lord was nailing to the wall of my mind would have read, "Wanted," showing my photo and name, and then the wording, "Reward! Amount to be determined."

At that point, I had no idea of the magnitude of the blessings that God had in store for us.

TRANSITIONS
Buying Plants

"Take the helmet of salvation and the sword of the Spirit, which is the Word of God"
Ephesians 6:17

The experience of buying plants for a new office would not seem to have any particular significance in this period of transition, but it did!

Letty had made the suggestion that my new office needed a lot of plants. Her thought was, "Plants will create a cheery atmosphere, and you are going to need that." How right she was! So, one afternoon during the time when we were putting our office together, we headed off to the nursery.

What stands out so vividly in this experience is the state of my emotions during this shopping trip. I had resigned from the security blanket of my former agency of 23 years. The experience of buying those plants seemed to bring a much deeper, and more fearful reality to what we were about to do. Feeling mesmerized into a state of half-consciousness, it was almost as though I wasn't even there.

While shopping, we ran smack dab into another agent who had been, and would continue to be, one of my competitors. Letty and I explained to him what we were about to do, and he very graciously and sincerely wished me good luck. But the experience of running into him raised my apprehension to another level. Anyone seeing me leaving that nursery would surely have thought, "That man looks like he is totally out of it; he's probably had one too many," as I stumbled along with a glazed look in my eyes.

But even in that state, I knew that the Lord was there. That knowledge is what kept me going; for at that point, it seemed to be the only reality in my thoughts.

Over the next few years our agency and our plants grew, and sure enough, sitting on the top of our metal file cabinets, the plants provided a cheery atmosphere to the office, just as Letty had predicted. She faithfully pruned and watered them, even though sometimes her "flow gauge" admittedly didn't work real well. When she watered the plants, she really watered them. And, just like our agency, they prospered.

A few years later, when we moved our office, we noticed large streaks of rust down the backs of our metal file cabinets. We both found this hilariously funny. We could just picture her dumping gallons and gallons of water into those plants as it ran up and over the tops of the planters and continued down the backs of the file cabinets. I remember telling her, "The city of Hamilton fire department could not have done it any better." Most of these cabinets are long gone, but we still have a couple of them, and every once in awhile I'll come across one of those rust spots. This always brings a chuckle, and a reminder of God's abundant and overflowing blessing in the early days of our new adventure.

TRANSITIONS
The Moment of Truth

"Take the helmet of salvation and the sword of the Spirit, which is the Word of God"
Ephesians 6:17

July 10, 1987, is a day that will remain etched in my memory forever.

We had been in business in our new agency for one month. That dense, black fog of fear and uncertainty continued to hang around outside the door of our office. On most days I was able to keep it outside. But, if it was one of those days when I was tired and more vulnerable to being easily discouraged, it would burst through a crack in my emotions. Once inside my thoughts, just like smoke billowing through a burning house, this anxiety would work its way deeper and deeper into the recesses of my mind. Such a day was July 10, 1987. On that morning I found myself both tired and discouraged.

Upon returning from a sales call that morning, I found one of those famous "pink slips" on my desk. Remember those? They were the "While You Were Out" slips, listing who had called and if there was a need for a return call. In this electronic age, these slips are no longer used, and I must admit that I really don't miss them.

That particular pink slip showed that a call had come in at 10:35 AM from my long-time friend, Jerry Jones. He had called to share "a word from the Lord today" which had come to him in his morning quiet time. The message said, "Read Deuteronomy 8:7-9. Then read Deuteronomy 8:10-20. Verse 18 is very, very important".

So I picked up my Bible, turned to these verses, and began to read. *"For the LORD your God is bringing you into a good land, a land with streams and pools of water, with springs flowing in the valleys and the hills; a land with wheat and barley, vines and fig trees, pomegranates, olive oil and honey; a land where bread will not be scarce and you will lack nothing."* Deuteronomy 8:7-9.

I continued on, reading Deuteronomy 8:10-20, just as Jerry had suggested. Verse 10 was a reminder to *"praise the LORD your God for the good land he has given you."*

Verse 18 was also a reminder, *"But remember the LORD your God, for it is he that gives you the ability to produce wealth, and so confirms his covenant, which he swore to your forefathers."*

Verse 19 gave a warning, *"If you ever forget the LORD your God and follow other gods and worship and bow down to them, I testify against you today that you will surely be destroyed."*

The impact of these words stopped me dead in my tracks. Just like that morning in Friendly's Restaurant two years before, I was mesmerized. I knew that God was speaking to me. Through his Word he was once again reassuring me about the future.

Time for the enemy to attack! And he did! Suddenly the doubts and the questions loomed large in my thoughts.

And then, the Moment of Truth! *The Moment of Truth!* I suddenly came face-to-face with the question, "Is this really true? Is God really going to do what his Word says, or is this just a passage of scripture to comfort me? Can I really, and I mean really, trust in the truth of these words?" I almost felt guilty even asking myself that question. At that moment I realized, that if I did not trust in the truth of these words, then the Christian faith is not real; it is just something to make us all feel better.

But deep within me I knew! I knew that my faith was real and that God's word was true. I knew down deep inside of me that the scriptures were truth. I just could not accept otherwise. I couldn't!

And then came this thought: "If I know that the scriptures really are God's Word, then I can trust the fact that the Lord used Jerry this morning to pass along his encouraging words about my future. I am being blessed by a visit from the Lord through his Word." I knew I should continue to move forward in faith."

Of course, as the years have gone on, I have been able to reflect on how God has fulfilled his promise. The joy brought to me by my career as an Independent Insurance Agent has exceeded my wildest expectations.

And, I am happy to say that I have never forgotten God's reminder to me in Deuteronomy 8:19-20. Every night when I leave my office, I thank him, and I praise him for all that he has done through his mighty hand.

Never will I ever forget the impact of that "Moment of Truth,"

TRANSITIONS
The Handle of the Sword

"Take the helmet of salvation and the sword of the Spirit, which is the Word of God"
Ephesians 6:17

In her inspiring book, *"On Eagle's Wings,"* Diana Stroh shares the following about what God's Word meant to her in her spiritual transition into a new and deeper relationship with Him:

"What an incredibly life-changing, amazing Book! All of a sudden it was not quite as overwhelming to me".

"The days when I took the time to sit down and open God's Word were huge steps in the right direction – in God's direction."

"It gave me clear direction and guidance and comforted me beyond anything I had previously tried. What took place between God, His Word, and me is nothing short of miraculous. Words cannot adequately describe what transpired between our spirits. I can shout from the rooftops that God's written Word is the primary tool he used to speak to me."

I share Diana's inspiring words, because they describe so well what God's Word meant to me in those early days of our new agency.

At that time the magnitude of the task ahead of my wife, Letty, and me would suddenly descend on me like a dense fog. There were so many unanswered questions. This was ground on which I had never walked before. The previous 23 years had been in a very secure and relatively stress-free environment.

It was as if my ship, which had been sailing peacefully along, had been sunk by a sudden storm. Now here I was beached on a totally unknown land looking at a totally foreign horizon and not really knowing which way to go forward.

At times, the fear and emotional loneliness of operating my own agency were almost paralyzing.

It was at those times that from within my thoughts would always emerge the reminder, that gentle reminder from God's Holy Spirit, that this was the right land to be in and that I was not alone.

God's reminder always came in the form of his Word, welling up from my subconscious mind and into the forefront of my thoughts. The various verses from the Psalms that I had committed to memory came to me, and I grabbed onto them and would not let them go. They were my lifeline. Without them I knew that I would sink.

There were several verses which seemed to form a "divine pattern", and I would repeat them over and over until the black clouds in my mind had been overcome. The handle of the sword began with Psalm 37:3-7:

> *Trust in the LORD and do good;*
> *dwell in the land and enjoy safe pasture.*
> *Delight yourself in the LORD*
> *and he will give you the desires of your heart.*
> *Commit your way to the LORD;*
> *trust in him and he will do this.*
> *He will make your righteousness shine like the dawn,*
> *the justice of your cause like the noonday sun.*
> *Be still before the LORD and wait patiently for him.*

Once again my thoughts progressed to Psalm 40:1-4. These were the same verses that God had given to me on that morning in Friendly's restaurant when he revealed to me that my dream of having my own agency would become a reality. It only seemed fitting that these verses would also become part of the handle of the sword, as they "picked up" right where Psalm 37:7 left off:

> *I waited patiently for the LORD;*
> *he turned to me and heard my cry.*
> *He lifted me out of the slimy pit,*
> *out of the mud and mire.*

he set my feet on a rock
and gave me a firm place to stand.
He put a new song in my mouth,
a hymn of praise to our God.
Many will see and fear
and put their trust in the LORD.
Blessed is the man
who makes the LORD his trust

My grip on the handle was further strengthened by Psalm 31:1-3

In you, O LORD, I have taken refuge;
let me never be put to shame;
deliver me in your righteousness.
Turn your ear to me,
come quickly to my rescue;
be my rock of refuge,
a strong fortress to save me.
Since you are my rock and my fortress,
for the sake of your name lead and guide me.

And finally, Psalm 32:8-10:

I will instruct you and teach you
in the way you should go;
I will counsel you and watch over you;
Do not be like the horse and mule,
which have no understanding
but must be controlled by bit and bridle
or they will not come to you.
Many are the woes of the wicked,
but the LORD's unfailing love
surrounds the man who trusts in him.

It was a divinely inspired "fit," and what a weapon it turned out to be! To this day, I marvel at how God put these verses together to give me that handle to grip, so that I could hold on to the Sword of His Spirit.

Diana Stroh's words say it so well. "What took place between God and me is nothing short of miraculous."

All praise and glory to Him.

TRANSITIONS
The Sheltering Tree

Any fireman will tell you that it is not always the fire which is the fatal element in a burning building, but rather the poison gases inherent in the smoke. Those gases are so poisonous that a few short breaths can render someone immediately unconscious.

Have you ever experienced fear that was almost paralyzing?

How well I remember such a moment. It happened in those early days of our new agency venture. It was as if our office was on fire that morning, bringing those billowing black clouds of smoke that choke the life out of any living thing that happens to be around. But those black clouds were not from the smoke of any fire, and they were not roiling around within the physical confines of our office. Rather, they were poisonous clouds of fear rolling over and over in my mind.

Externally, everything that morning was pretty much as it had been the day before and even the day before that. Yes, our cash flow was tight, but it had been that way for several months. We faced no particular challenges that morning, other than what had confronted us at other times. So, outwardly things were pretty much the same.

But within my mind, some sort of storm had apparently been brewing, because suddenly, out of nowhere the black clouds of fear swooped down upon me like the heat of a flash fire.

All of the fears and uncertainties inherent in the beginning of our new venture seemed to come together. Like the stampede of wild animals on the African plain, all of those worries and anxieties seemed to be running wild and trampling me into the ground.

The emotional paralysis was so frightening that I suddenly felt powerless to move.

My first instinct was to reach for my phone and call my wife, Letty Ellen, but I couldn't even move to pick up the phone. If my life had depended upon calling 911 at that moment, I would not have been able to do it. Even my memory bank of scripture had shut down.

Those few moments seemed like an eternity.

With my head buried in my arms, I felt something underneath me. It turned out to be a stack of unopened mail that had come earlier that morning. Ever so slowly I picked up the top envelope, opened it, and began to read what was inside. It was a copy of a poem that had come out of a devotional book entitled *"The Sheltering Tree."* As I began to read it, the words began to lift my spirits. By the end of the first two pages, the words seemed to be like the sunlight emerging in an opening through the black cloud of fear that had overwhelmed me.

At the end of the poem was this handwritten note: "Thank you, J.D., for being my sheltering tree!" My dear friend, Lamont Jacobs, "Jake," had written those words. Tears of joy and relief flowed across my arms and down onto the pile of mail underneath me. Those words have since taken on immortality in my memory because of the impact they had on me that day.

When I regained my composure, I called Jake. I shared with him how timely his words were and how they had rescued me from the pit of despair. He shared with me, "You know, when I was reading this as part of my devotions the other morning, I had the strongest prompting to send it to you, and to put that little note on the bottom of it. Now I know why, J.D."

Was this just another coincidence? No! There are no coincidences when God is involved. In our "worldly" way of trying to explain things, we tend to put that label on situations like this. But when we do that, we dismiss the precious dimension of His divine, supernatural power that is always at work when we look to Him.

TRANSITIONS
The Flood

Little did we know when we built our home in 1972 that it was being constructed on a flood plain. At that time, flood maps were very unsophisticated and ordinances concerning construction in those areas were few and far between.

Ironically, what sold us on the lot in the first place, was the day that Letty sat down on the bank of Pleasant Run Creek and put her feet in the water. I still remember the realtor who was with us saying, "I think you folks have just bought yourselves a lot." He was right! That lot was purchased. The house went up, and we lived happily ever after. Well, almost!

Pleasant Run Creek is just that – most of the time. This very clean stream is fed by various underground springs, so it always has water rippling over the rocks in various places. With trees growing up along its banks, it is very picturesque, and it makes for an attractive feature at the rear of every yard along its banks. It drains a large area of northern Hamilton County and meanders its way through the city of Fairfield.

However, during periods of very heavy rain it cannot hold all of the water which drains into it from a very large area. Coupled with the fact that the course of the stream is a gradual descent to the Miami River, this makes for a lot of water overflowing its banks and running downhill at a very fast pace. Enter the ideal scenario for flash flooding.

This is where almost living happily ever after comes in to play. The first flood occurred in 1979. We eventually cleaned everything up and life went on as usual. The worst part of this scenario, however, is not the cleanup. It is that lingering fear that remains and then rears its ugly head whenever there is a hard rain in a short period of time.

I share all of this because it provides the backdrop for what happened during the next flood. It occurred in the summer of 1989, a short two years into our new agency. One dark night the thunder began to roar, the lightning cracked, the winds whipped up, and it looked as if we had a storm on our hands that had the same capability as the one in 1979. It raged on for about three hours or so and was still going strong past midnight. At a time like this there isn't much one can do except pray and get the shakes. Looking out the window in the dark of night revealed water swirling around everywhere. The awful roar as it rushed through our backyard sounded like Niagara Falls.

Then it happened. The water began to fill the garage. It entered under the wall between the garage and the kitchen. A line of muddy water worked its way across the kitchen floor and into the family room. You could feel the "squish" under your feet as it worked its way through the carpeting of the family room and down the hall into the first bedroom.

I had a feeling of total helplessness, and I remember thinking, "Father, with all the business pressures, I just can't handle another threat to our home."

That night seemed like an eternity. But finally, morning began to break through. The rain had stopped. Going outside revealed that the water had subsided, but it had left a film of mud over everything. Walking back into the kitchen, I picked up the phone in an effort to find some help to deal with the muddy mess.

In my business we deal with claim situations like this quite frequently. Despite my experience however, I was unable to make contact with any of the water restoration contractors that we normally used. At that moment, standing there in the mud on our kitchen floor, I felt like the loneliest man in the world! As I opened the phone book and leafed through the Yellow Pages, I cried out, "Father, I feel so alone! Please send somebody to help us. Then, finally, on the very next phone call came a pleasant voice on the other end. In fact, it was so pleasant, that at first I thought it must be a recording. I remember asking, "Is this a real person?" "Yes," came the reply. After relaying how desperate I was, I will never ever forget his response, "We will be there in two hours."

As I opened the door from the house into the garage and raised the garage door, I will never forget what happened next. There in the back yard, in a huge mud puddle, were four mallard ducks. Quack! Quack! Quack! Quack! In the midst of all of this devastation they were playing and flapping around in that puddle as if they didn't have a care in the world. And, I don't suppose they did!

For some reason this seemed hilarious to me, and I found myself laughing so hard I lost my balance on the slippery mud of the garage floor and down I went! Sitting up in the mud watching those ducks suddenly put the whole scenario into the right perspective. The humor brought on by that scene just lifted the burden of it completely off of my shoulders. I remember saying to myself, "Father, you do have a sense of humor." I knew! I just knew he had sent those ducks. There was no other explanation for their being in my yard at just that time. From my desperate cry to him for help, first came that reassuring voice on the phone, and then, the ducks! I was no longer alone.

I share this experience because it truly touched my heart. I believe it was yet another example of God's divine intervention during those early years of our transition into our new agency.

TRANSITIONS

PART II
The Journaling Journey

TRANSITIONS
How It All Began

My journaling journey started with a sermon tape from Dr. Charles Stanley entitled "Biblical Meditation." In that message, Dr. Stanley stressed the importance of reading slowly through the scriptures and allowing your thoughts to develop, listening to what meaning the Lord might have for you in a passage at that particular time in your walk with Him.

At various times over the years, Dr. Stanley, and my other hero in the faith, Dr. Chuck Swindoll, had both emphasized the value of writing down your prayer requests and then recording the Lord's answers to those requests. Although that idea appealed to me, I always felt it would require too much effort, and I would be too busy to do it.

Well, somewhere along the line, I found myself getting up a little earlier, brewing the coffee, and then settling in to my favorite chair with the Word in front of me. Alongside me with the scriptures was a simple 8 1/2 X 11 spiral notebook.

As I read and reflected on the Word, I began to record the thoughts that came to me, and I found myself actually praying to the Father through the words that were being recorded in my notebook.

Gradually, I began to notice that writing down my thoughts was not the tedious task I had thought it would be. In fact, to my surprise, many times my thoughts just seemed to "glide" onto the pages as I was writing them down.

Sometimes my writing would go on for an hour or longer, and before I realized it, I would realize I had written one page, a second page, and anywhere from three to ten pages in my notebook.

People who are able to pray for long periods of time had always amazed me. No matter how hard I had tried, when I prayed aloud, my thoughts would begin to wander off to some totally unrelated subject. This, of course was very frustrating. I would become so discouraged about trying to pray to the Lord for any more than five minutes. Some "prayer warrior" I was!

One of the wonderful discoveries I made was, that while I was writing down the thoughts from my meditations, my mind remained focused on what I was praying about. I was no longer becoming distracted. Writing down my thoughts enabled me to stay on course, and for longer periods of time that I had ever thought possible.

An hour could go by before I knew it. What, *me* – able to pray for an hour? As amazed as I was, I realized that praying for an extended period of time was now a reality for me. Many were the times when I just kept on writing and praying, oblivious to the time involved.

And that is how it all began.

TRANSITIONS
The Value Of Journaling

Over the fifteen-plus years on this journaling journey, I have made several wonderful discoveries.

Getting Up and Getting Going

After a while, my first thought upon waking each morning, was no longer that I didn't want to get out of bed. Rather, on many mornings I found that I couldn't wait to get a cup of coffee and sit down with the Word and my notebook in my lap, to fellowship with the Lord and see what he had to say to me.

To my complete surprise, the choice of whether to stay in bed for another hour or to get up and get into my quiet time with the Lord, became a no-brainer. Early on, and I'm reluctant to admit this, I never would have guessed that this would be the case.

Looking Back at God's Hand

Many times, while reflecting back to prior notebooks and the entry made on a particular day, I was blown away by what I was reading. The content of some of those entries had me asking myself, "Where did *that* come from?" In those cases, it was obvious to me that I was just not capable, in my own mortal mind, of composing such meaningful thoughts.

I firmly believe that God will share meaningful thoughts with any of us, if we will just stop and take the opportunity to spend quiet one-on-one time with him.

A journal can enable each of us to have a written record, a chronicle if you will, of the profound and encouraging thoughts that God has intended to uniquely bring our way. Can you imagine how encouraging this is, knowing that God has spoken personally to you? Can you imagine just how *real* this makes him become in our lives?

God's Glossary

A journal provides a glossary of thoughts that just may be needed on any particular day. I refer to this as "God's Glossary."

There were many mornings when I came before the Lord burdened by some particular matter. It may have been a financial or a health-related matter; it may have been complications in a relationship or just flat-out fear about the future. These and other matters sometimes felt overwhelming and discouraging.

During these moments of apprehension, I would find myself going back into one of my notebooks from a recent month or even from several years ago. Finding the words on those pages hitting dead-center into the issue over which I had been so discouraged was more encouraging and uplifting that I can properly describe. After this had happened a few times, I began to realize that it was the Holy Spirit who was so lovingly taking me back to a prior meditation which addressed my concern that day.

The earlier entry, recorded days, months or even years before, often related exactly to my apprehension of that current morning and provided the encouragement I needed to face it and to move on. This happened too many times to be coincidence. How encouraging this was to see first-hand how faithful the Lord is to us.

Folks have asked me the obvious question from time to time, "How do you know these thoughts are not simply a figment of your own vivid, worldly imagination on any given morning?"

Perhaps some of these thoughts might well have been from my own imagination on a given day, depending on how "tuned in" I happened to be at the time. However, I know, I just know that much of what I recorded came from the Lord. But, don't just take my word for it. Try it yourself!

Is journaling for everybody? Probably not! But I would encourage you to try it to see for yourself if it can be a medium through which the Lord will make his loving and faithful presence so real to you.

You don't need a hardback book with the word "Journal" printed on the front cover, although if it is what you prefer, that's fine. A simple spiral notebook will do. Fill one up and then go on to another one. I have found it beneficial to date and number the pages, as this becomes helpful for future reference.

My friend, if you decide to try journaling, I pray that you will be enriched by the experience. For me it has truly been "A Journey of Joy."

I wish you well!

John Dodsworth
January 20, 2012

TRANSITIONS

⊱━◈━➤━◉━◂━◈━⊰

PART III
Sharing The Meditations
A Journey of Joy

TRANSITIONS
The Joy of Knowing

Father, all through this Journal you have revealed to me just how personal you really are. Down through the years, through this endeavor you have shared so many wonderful thoughts and insights to me.

When I read and reflect back to the meditations of past mornings and see what has been written down, I know that such thoughts can only come from you.

What encouragement that brings to me.

It is so wonderful to know that I can have this kind of conversation with you, the Omnipotent God of the Universe.

I will never ever fully understand it, but I *know, I know!* I thank you for this *knowing* and for the wonderful sense of joy that it brings to me.

In the name of Jesus, I thank you, and I praise you.

Oh, what a wonderful mystery this all is.

TRANSITIONS
A Blank State of Mind

Father, as I sit here this morning, my mind feels "blank," with so many thoughts running in and out, none of them staying long enough to establish residency. It seems like nothing is there.

I guess I should just focus on being thankful that I am so comforted by your presence, knowing that I can actually come to you with what I perceive to be a blank state of mind. Even that perception does not hinder my wanting to be here with you. Even now I know that your Holy Spirit is here with me. I feel no guilt. I am totally at peace with this situation. Your love, Father, is so strong that it permeates even these times when my mind feels blank.

Well, so much for dwelling on the perceived blank state of my mind, for when I think about it, my mind is *not* really "blank" this morning. If it was, I couldn't be recording these thoughts, could I?

The conclusion is so obvious that it makes me wonder about my thought process here.

I realize that I do not always have to come before you with an agenda, with some kind of spiritual format. Rather it is much better to come before you with an open heart, joyful just to be with you, and to be open to whatever your Holy Spirit wants to say to me.

And then, to have the ability to be able to record these thoughts you have given me in my journal, I am blessed, Father – *blessed!*

In the Name of Jesus, I thank you.

TRANSITIONS
Victory Through Grace

I love these morning times with you, Father!

Sometimes, though, I feel as if my heart isn't "right" enough to come before you. But your faithful and wonderful Holy Spirit reminds me of your grace that is mine through my Lord and Savior, Jesus Christ, and that in him your door is always open to me.

So, I come before you, mindful of my imperfections, really, just flat out mindful of the sin in my life. There, I said it, *sin!*

I am also mindful of your grace and forgiveness that is promised in your Word, and of how loving and accepting you are of a repentant heart.

I can see why it would be so easy at this point in my walk of faith to have a pity party, to stop and dwell on my mistakes and failures, thinking how unworthy I am to even be in your Holy Presence.

This becomes a crucial point in my journey of faith. If I stop going forward in my walk, if I choose to dwell on my sins and failures, focusing inwardly instead of outwardly, then I am really turning my back on all of your promises, Father; I am failing to accept your grace and forgiveness, turning my back on the sacrifice that was made for me by my Lord Jesus.

Oh, how subtle this rejection becomes; how the enemy uses it to block the flow of your power into my life, stopping and preventing the advancement toward the life of victory that brings glory praise and honor to you.

And yet, it is at this point, as I recognize my unworthiness and bring you my repentant heart, that I become most worthy in your eyes.

In accepting your forgiveness, my relationship with you takes on an even stronger dimension. Through my forgiven heart, your peace and your power begin to flow again, bringing the victorious life that reflects glory, praise and honor to you. Father, I am so thankful that I know this truth. I know it because I have experienced it.

I bring before you, Lord, all of those folks who have stopped at the terminal of doubt and self-pity in their lives, and I pray that they would get on the train of your grace, accepting the free ride, that wonderful ride of freedom and adventure which brings victory into their lives just as it was intended to be.

I can understand what the Apostle Paul means when he refers to himself as "chief among sinners." And yet, I look at what you accomplished through him, and the adventurous life that he led as he made the journey that was chosen for him. What an encouragement this is.

In the name of Jesus, I thank you, and I praise you.

TRANSITIONS
All the Little Miracles

I am out on the patio this morning, listening to the ripple and gurgle of our "Moses Rock." This is such a peaceful and refreshing sound within the backdrop of the morning silence.

Not a leaf rustles. Even the sea oats barely move. Morning has its own rhythm, a serene and peaceful ambiance, as if to portend the wonderful opportunities and possibilities inherent within the coming day.

All of this is your creation, Father. All of it is part of your divine rhythm. Within that divine rhythm is the anticipation of the day that lies ahead, full of uplifting and joyful experiences, full of loving relationships, full of disappointments, full of temporary setbacks, full of victories, full of blessings that are more than we could ever anticipate. All of these things are the little miracles that are occurring all around us everyday.

Winter's cold has left us for awhile, giving way to the warmer days, to the beauty and color of blooming flowers and the lush green of new grass. The blossoms on the trees become a little more mature each day, sending a message that summer is drawing closer. It is a time of renewal within nature's rhythm.

As I opened my eyes from this morning's prayer, the sun of this new day suddenly shone across the pages of my journal.

All of these things are part of the little miracles that occur around us everyday.

Psalm 111:2 reminds us, *"Great are the works of the LORD; they are pondered by all who delight in them."*

In the Name of Jesus, I thank you, and I praise you.

TRANSITIONS
Back to the Basics

Meditating on John 15-17, has been so helpful these past few days, Father. I feel like I have gone "back to basics." This is so comforting and encouraging.

The war within me rages on! The temptations, pressures and concerns that attack my mind seem at times to be so overwhelming that they are like an African jungle stampede, trying to trample me by the weight of their numbers, the dust from their pounding hooves swirling around in my head, clouding my judgment. The pace and direction of my thoughts resembles those stampeding animals as they run wildly with no sense of direction.

Within the roar and confusion of this scene I subtly slip into the trap of trying to figure everything out, looking for answers within my own thought processes. The Apostle Paul's words ring so loudly in my mind, *"What a wretched man I am! Who will rescue me from this body of death? Thanks be to God through Jesus Christ our Lord!"* Romans 7:24-25.

I am blessed to know this truth; that I am not defenseless. I have your Word as my sword, the weapon that has the power of your Holy Spirit, the weapon that no enemy can ever stand against.

Hear O Lord, and answer me,
for I am poor and needy.
Guard my life, for I am devoted to you.
You are my God;
save your servant who trusts in you.

Have mercy on me, O LORD,
for I call to you all day long.
Bring joy to your servant,
for to you, O LORD,
I lift up my soul."
Psalm 86:1-4

Father, to me this is going "back to basics," back to what always works. Your divine rhythm stills the stampede of my thoughts. There is order! There is peace! There is victory! And in this victory, is a life that brings glory, praise and honor to you.

TRANSITIONS
Strengthening Those Spiritual Muscles

As the morning unfolded, the economic news received was not exactly what I had hoped for. My commission statement is down again, to one of the lowest amounts I have had in months.

After getting that news, I was informed through another email that I have lost another long-time account. This seems to have become a trend over the past several months. This has never happened before to the extent that it has been happening lately. And the business I have lost is from clients who have been with me for many years.

For the first time in recent memory, I am beginning to wonder what the future holds for me in this career that I have loved so much. I know I should not feel this way, but I feel helpless as to what to do to retain those long-time accounts that have historically always been so loyal. My concerns are so strong that they are blocking any creative effort to come up with a plan to deal with this situation. Hope seems to be totally missing from my "solar system."

And then,I reached across my desk and picked up one of my journals that just happened to be lying there. As I began to read through some of those entries they began to minister to me. And, I had to smile, for my heart was suddenly uplifted by the words in those entries. Reading them lifted my spirits, and I felt my hope returning. This was totally unexpected.

Suddenly my focus was not on the seeming impossibility of my circumstances, but my hope was back on you, Lord Jesus, right where it needs to be. I have been in this situation so many times before, and you have always uplifted me and given me the strength to go on. The phrase that seems to ring in my heart is "the strengthening of my spiritual muscles." These are the "muscles" that strengthen my relationship with you, Father.

Thank you for being so faithful!

Thank you for being so faithful.

TRANSITIONS
Freedom vs. Fear

If ever there was a "home game," this is it!

Father, I thank you that I am no longer afraid of unanswered questions or the uncertainty of the future. While I still have strong concerns, and those fears that sneak up on me once in awhile, you have taken away the deep intensity of sub-conscious fear that has had my thoughts and emotions in its vice-like grip for the past several years.

Never will I ever forget the fear that gripped me in the early summer of 1987 when we started our agency, with no clients and very few financial resources. On the horizon, all we could seem to see were the goblins of uncertainty attacking us on all fronts. How vividly I remember a fear that almost paralyzed me. I remember that morning when I was so gripped by fear that I could not even pick up my telephone.

The only light of encouragement I could see on that awful horizon of uncertainty was your Word. I held so tightly to the "Sword of Your Spirit." It was my only weapon to slash through the tangled vines of those destructive thoughts that were always closing in on me, as if to choke out all light of hope.

Moment by moment, hour by hour, day by day, I remember repeating over and over, the passages from your Word that lifted my spirits. Those passages constantly reminded me that you were always with me.

Gradually, as the power in your Word grew stronger in my thoughts, the grip of those fears began to subside. I will never forget that memorable afternoon in July of the following year when it hit me! Suddenly, I realized that I was no longer afraid. I remember being almost mesmerized by that overwhelming sense of peace that came over me. I was no longer afraid! I was no longer afraid! I was free of that awful sense of fear that had gripped me so deeply. Even today, I cannot explain it. But the reality of it has stayed with me; the joy of that moment has never left me.

Father, I thank you that in the freedom from that fear was born a sense of the adventure there is in knowing and following you. This is the ultimate adventure in this life – knowing the joy, knowing you are always with me, knowing you are able to do all things, knowing I don't have to understand the how of it, of how it all works.

My part is just to accept it through faith in Christ Jesus, allowing your Holy Spirit to penetrate into my thoughts by thinking and meditating on your Word.

Freedom from fear!

Oh, what a wonderful mystery this is.

TRANSITIONS
The Beacon

So-o-o-o quiet – so very, very quiet here this morning!

Father, even though my mind is wandering all over the place and my thoughts are all jumbled, I still know your faithful presence; I know the truth in your Word.

Through your faithful presence, you continue to show me that no circumstances in my life can change this truth. The storm clouds of financial pressure, of broken relationships that need to be repaired, of the uncertainties in our nation's future – none of these can change the truth in your Word. How many times I have had to remind myself that neither the strength nor the weakness of my cash flow affects the truth in your Word.

And yet, I can very easily feel compelled to try to "fix" all of these areas of concern. The pace of my life then moves faster and faster. It becomes so easy to be "too busy" to spend my morning quiet time with you in your Word. I start thinking that I have to hurry to the office because I have so much to do. I allow myself to become a slave to the mindset that I must always be trying to catch up. What an empty goal that becomes. What does "catching up" mean most of the time anyway?

Ever so subtly I lose my sense of direction. And when I lose it, do I stop and contemplate just where I am going? Do I even think of looking in your direction for answers, for guidance? Sadly, all too often I try on my own to find my way. The results are confusion, fatigue and discouragement. I can so easily find myself on the enemy's "home field," where he is a heavy favorite, and I am a definite underdog. On his field, the fans of confusion, fatigue and discouragement are all around me with their thunderous roar.

But does any of this change your Word? Romans 8:38-39 reminds us: "*...neither death nor life, neither angels nor demons, neither the present nor the future, nor any powers, neither height nor depth nor anything else in all creation, will be able to separate us from the love of God that is in Christ Jesus our Lord.*" There are many such reminders throughout the New Testament.

My thoughts this morning seem to typify the current unclear direction of my life. Lately, at times I have felt like a man wandering in the wilderness. My sense of direction for my life is not clear. And yet, I know that I am the one who has moved. You, Lord, have not moved. The truth in your Word remains like a beacon in the fog. It is immovable.

I know that I must seek your truth each and every day. Yesterday's truth, while firm and eternal, somehow never seems to have the momentum to carry me through a new day. But, it does remind me where to look! May I make a conscious choice each day to make your truth be my beacon. May the beam of light from your Word shine through the fog of my muddled thoughts and guide me away from the shoals into calm waters.

In the name of Jesus, I thank you, and I praise you.

TRANSITIONS
A Beautiful Day – A Gift in Time

Today is a beautiful, clear, sunny spring morning.

The flowers seem to look up to the sun as if in eager anticipation of another day to bloom brighter and brighter. The tulips seem to spread their colorful petals as if to coax more sunlight into their centers. Even the bright yellow flowers of the dandelions seem bigger and brighter in the morning sun. The bubbling water from the Moses Rock is the only sound to permeate the rhythm of the morning stillness.

I praise you for this day, Father, your marvelous creation, infinite in its beauty, regal in its splendor, so warm, so inviting, so uplifting, so filled with the promise of good things.

It is ours to enjoy. This is a day on the calendar that will never come again.

Today is a day which will have its own unique opportunities for bringing praise to you within all that we do. For you are to be praised, Father, no matter what situations may arise. Be they positive or otherwise, all glory, praise and honor are to be yours this beautiful day.

TRANSITIONS
Forgiveness In The Trenches

Father, good morning!

When I reflect back on yesterday's thoughts that you shared with me, I am so aware of my sin, of my drifting away from you. Only hours later, that very same afternoon I lost my cool with some good people in my office who were only trying to do their jobs!

Yesterday morning, I wrote the following to you in my journal: "In gratitude to you for all that you are and do for me, may I be obedient to you by focusing my thinking, my thoughts, constantly on your Word."

I said that to you, and I honestly and sincerely meant it.

And then, later that morning a very unusual and unavoidable situation occurred. The flow of my day was suddenly interrupted – and not in the right direction!

And what did I do? In a tense situation I allowed myself to focus entirely on the circumstances, on the "how" and "why" of it. My concern was about how much money this was going to cost us and how inconvenient this was to me. I took my "spiritual eyes" off of you, Lord, and put them entirely on the circumstances.

Here I was, in a high-pressure moment when my conduct could have honored you, and I failed! I absolutely failed! My anger prevailed!

What kind of man am I that I would do that?

In the name of Jesus, I ask you to forgive me, Father. And I thank you, that as I make this confession to you, I know that you have not turned away from me and that through your wonderful grace you have forgiven me. *"If we confess our sins, he is faithful and just and will forgive us our sins and purify us from all unrighteousness."* (1 John 1:9)

Father, I am in awe of you, of how you provide peace and an ongoing joy in the midst of circumstances where the enemy is trying to separate me from your presence.

Now what remains is for me to ask for forgiveness from those folks who were on the receiving end of my tirade.

Postscript: They did!

TRANSITIONS
Thoughts Under Seige

There doesn't seem to be any particular concentration of thought for me this morning, Father.

I got up this morning with all good intentions of talking with you, of getting into your Word and meditating on it and yet, I feel besieged, almost overwhelmed with temptations, confusion and emptiness.

I confess this to you because I know that this is me... me! You have not changed, you have not moved, and I find great comfort in that.

I feel like a man who is clawing his way up the cliff, only to slide back, leaving ridges in the rock, the ridges left by my fingers as I try desperately to stop the downward slide.

And yet, even as I seem to be sliding down the mountain, I know! I know that you are there, Father, that my Lord Jesus has made it possible for your grace to open a channel in my heart for me to receive the flow of the strength and power of your Holy Spirit.

Each day seems to have its own climb up that mountain. Each day has its gaps. Yesterday's climb will not do for today. Each day must bring a new reminder of your grace and forgiveness. For then, your power flows! When I choose to tune into that power, the attack is overcome.

Therein lies the victory over the daily siege of confusion, temptation and emptiness.

TRANSITIONS
A Divine Rhythm

There's a song from the musical "Oklahoma" entitled, "Oh What a Beautiful Morning," brought to my mind, Father, by winter in its finest beauty this morning. The steady, gentle fall of snow has a peaceful rhythm, a rhythm which reminds me not to hurry.

The snow falls gently and still covers the ground. Its rhythm can bring a one inch snow, a ten inch snow, or whatever depth you would have it be. But, no matter what the depth, it happens with the same rhythm. It is peaceful, gentle and steady. It does not hurry to the ground to bring a greater depth in a shorter period of time, because it doesn't have to.

Nor do we in the pace of our everyday lives have to "hurry," to work "faster," so that we can accomplish more and more in less and less time – a rhythm governed by the pace of the world around us.

The "rhythm of the world," or your rhythm, Father, – the "rhythm of the snow;" I do have a choice as to which rhythm will govern my day.

Why would I not choose your rhythm with its peaceful yet steady pace? Yours is a pace which brings peace and encouragement through the constant reassurance of your divine presence. This is the pace that also brings that which I covet the most; and that is your wisdom, your divine discernment.

Thank you for these insights this morning.

May all praise, glory and honor be to you, Father, today and every day.

TRANSITIONS
Strength For The Walk

Father, I echo the prayer put forth by the Apostle Paul in Colossians 1:9-12, and I ask you to fill me *"...with the knowledge of your will, through all spiritual wisdom and understanding."* I pray this *"... in order that I may live a life worthy of you, O Lord, pleasing you in every way, bearing fruit in every good work and growing in my knowledge of you, O God, being strengthened with all power according to your glorious might, so that I may have great endurance and patience, and joyfully, give thanks to you, Father, you who have qualified me to share in the inheritance of the saints in the kingdom of light."*

Father, in my own human comprehension, I can't begin to know the depth of this meaning, for this depth is endless in my relationship with you in Christ Jesus. I ask you to give me your wisdom, your divine discernment and your courage, so that I will press forward in faith and not listen to the doubts that creep into my thoughts.

Through your Holy Spirit, instill in me your compassion and your love, so that I may be sensitive to the needs of those around me, and to be able to encourage them as you encourage me.

I claim this promise in your Word, *"You, O Sovereign LORD, are my strength. you make my feet like the feet of a deer. You enable me to go on the heights."* (Habakkuk 3:19)

Father, may the truth in these words ring loudly within my thoughts today. May my walk bring glory, praise and honor to you.

TRANSITIONS
Comfort

Psalm 62:1-2

My soul finds rest in you alone, O God

There is no earthly plan or pattern, no system or procedure, no activity, – nothing that gives me the peace and the rest that comes to me through your Word, Father. Thank you!

My salvation comes from you

Only through the shed blood, the sacrifice of your Son, my Lord and Savior, Jesus Christ, can I have eternal residence, an eternal relationship with you. Only in and through you, Lord Jesus, am I fit to come before the Father. Thank you, Lord Jesus, for dying for me, for all the suffering that you went through for me, for all of us.

Thank you, Father, for the sacrifice that you made, sending your only Son, so that we could have eternal fellowship with you.

You alone are my rock and my salvation,
You are my fortress,
I will never be shaken.

Only you alone, Father, in the power of your Holy Spirit have the power to keep me from being shaken. Yours is the only power strong enough to penetrate even the darkest fears that are put forth by the enemy.

What comfort this brings to me, Father, this "rest" that can only be found in you. Resting in you comes from thinking on your Word. Thinking on your Word activates your Holy Spirit who then brings peace and power into my day. What comfort I find in knowing and experiencing these things.

Oh, what a wonderful mystery this all is!

TRANSITIONS
On Being Tired

Father, I am struggling this morning. I can't seem to stay awake or to concentrate. Is it the lack of coffee (no filters) or food (no breakfast)??

If it is, shame on me that I would not make the most of this opportunity to be with you.

I am almost afraid to give into it by putting how I feel into words. Giving a verbal affirmation to my feelings, makes me think that I am somehow "admitting defeat." But, no! My foolish pride is playing tricks on my thought patterns which just happen to be vulnerable from fatigue this morning.

And so, I will freely admit that I feel worn out! I feel exhausted!

Was it cleaning out the garage yesterday that did it? What?

Tired or not, I do know this; without your strength this day will be lost to me... lost! And I do not want to waste even one day in my life. If I go ahead and write off this day in my own mind, then gone forever are the opportunities that it will offer.

You did not intend for us to live this way. Tired or not makes no difference in the truth and power that is in your Word. Tired or not, if I make a conscious choice to recall from memory those thoughts stored up from your Word, the power of your Holy Spirit will be activated. This day can then become a day of victory and not defeat.

Being tired does not have to rob me of a day of victory in my life. A day of victory brings joy. This joy brings glory to you.

This is really my choice, isn't it?

TRANSITIONS
Retreat and Victory

Lately, it seems as though my temptations, doubts, and fearful concerns are winning every skirmish. The battle line in my life seems to be pushing backward, and these thoughts seem to be conquering more and more territory in my life.

It is as if I look over the parapet in the fortress of my mind, and I see them attacking. But, rather than use the weapon of your Word, I jump down from the parapet and retreat without even swinging my sword at the enemy.

And then, no victory! There is never a victory when there is retreat. The resulting emptiness is almost devastating.

There is no pattern to what I am doing. Everything seems to be at loose ends. You seem to be "off in the distance," Father, not because you have moved, but because I have moved. I have retreated in the battle rather than standing firm in your Word.

Why? Why would a man ever retreat in the face of certain victory? Why would a man allow himself to experience emptiness when the riches of your divine fellowship are there for the taking?

As the Apostle Paul says, *"What a wretched man I am! Who will rescue me from this body of death?"*(Romans 7:24). And yet, I know... I know the truth of Paul's words that follow that admission, *"Thanks be to God through Christ Jesus our Lord!"*(Romans 7:25)

Without your sword, Father, I am defenseless. With it, I am victorious.

This battle becomes an adventure. Knowing that victory is certain makes it an adventure to be sought after and embraced not only because it brings joy to my life, but also because it brings glory, praise, and honor to you.

TRANSITIONS
My Psalm Of Praise For Your Creation

My Psalm of Praise for Your Creation

Good morning, Father! I wish to offer you this psalm today.

I praise you for who you are,
more omnipotent, more powerful, more loving
than my mortal, human mind can comprehend.

Only you can bring the refreshing rains that make the grass
so green, that enable the trees to grow and the flowers to bloom.

Only you can make the beauty of the pink Mandeville,
a pink so vibrant that words cannot do its beauty justice.

Only you can make the sounds of rippling waters,
those gentle soothing sounds that can quiet the heart.

Only you can make the mighty waterfall,
its thunderous awesome sounds as it cascades over the edge.
And yet, even within its thunder, there is beauty,
and, a reassurance of your awesome power.

Only you can bring the tides,
so rhythmically and so constantly to and from the shore;
a reminder of your faithful presence.

Only you can make the majesty of a snow-capped mountain,
and the awesome splendor of its reflection in the lake that lies at
its base.

Only you can make the stillness of Splitrock Bay,
and the rock formations that form its channel.

Your creation, Father, shouts loudly of your divine presence
evident in the intense beauty of all you have created.

Father, in the name of Jesus, I offer you my psalm this morning, in honor of, and in appreciation for the awesome beauty and splendor of all of your creation.

TRANSITIONS
New Dawn – New Hope

*Send forth your light and your truth, let them guide me; let them bring me to your holy
mountain, to the place where you dwell.*
Psalm 43:3

Father, your "holy mountain" is always within me, in my heart, in my
thoughts, when I choose to dwell on your Word.

As I look outside this morning, I see two layers in the dawn as
it breaks into a new day. I see the darkness of the surface; the trees
and houses silhouetted against the light in the sky above them. Their
outlines are barely discernible in the morning darkness. But the sky
soon gets brighter with each passing moment, until the emerging light
overcomes the darkness. The surface outlines become brighter and
brighter as the dawn unfolds, bringing a day of bright sunshine that
lingers over all.

Father, this reminds me of the hope that you always bring to me
when I allow your Word to penetrate my thoughts. Just as the dawn
brings the light of a new day, your Word brings your Holy Spirit into
my heart. Your Holy Spirit always brings hope. This hope always
overcomes any darkness, any doubt, any fear that lurks within my
heart and my thoughts.

Father, just as the emerging daylight enables me to see the houses,
the trees, the grass, all of the details that make up that "surface layer," so
it is the same with the light from your Holy Spirit. Your light enables me
to focus on the opportunities that shine brighter and brighter through
the darkness of the doubts in my thoughts. When I start to doubt the

success of our business, new clients come our way, or we get a compliment from someone about the service that we have provided for them.

Just as the dawn breaks and the light becomes brighter every morning, so do your love and faithfulness.

Oh, what a wonderful mystery this all is.

TRANSITIONS
It Never Fails

The quiet of the morning! No one is up yet, and the soothing, steady sound of the falling rain is so restful, so peaceful – an ongoing reminder of your rhythm in our lives and what it can mean... if only we would give you the time, Father.

You want only to bless us; your Word makes that so clear. You are so very, very faithful.

By day, the LORD, directs his love, at night his song is with me, a prayer to the God of my life. (Psalm 42:8)

As the deer pants for streams of water, so my soul pants for you, O God. My soul thirsts for God, for the living God. When can I go and meet with God? (Psalm 41:1-2)

I am blessed to know the answer to that question, for I have your Word through which your Holy Spirit always speaks to my heart. It focuses my thoughts on you, Lord Jesus, on you, Father God.

Never does it fail to give me your peace!

Never does it fail to give me your strength!

Never does it fail to lift my spirits!

Never does it fail to make me aware of your faithfulness!

Never does it fail to remind me just how near you are!

Never does it fail to give me your power!

Never does it fail to encourage me to press on, no matter what the circumstances!

Never does it fail to impart your wisdom, your discernment, to me, that which I covet above all else!

Never does it fail to remind me how much you love me!

Never does it fail to remind me that I have the freedom to ask you for anything, anything in the Name of Jesus!

What a blessed man I am, Father!

TRANSITIONS
A Father's Day Gift

4AM

This is Father's Day. It looks like I am going to get an early start.

Father, maybe on this special day it is fitting that I get an early start to find my way out of the spiritual wasteland where in recent weeks my temptations have been trying to grab center stage in my emotions.

Why am I always tempted to want to look ahead? Why does my imagination always try to create scenarios of fearful things to come; thoughts of getting back at someone who has offended me; thoughts that are lustful; thoughts that seem to center only on me? All of this internal conflict has me wandering around in a desert of spiritual emptiness.

The Apostle Paul puts it so well in Romans 7:21-24: *"When I want to do good, evil is right there with me. For in my inner being, I delight in God's law, but I see another law at work in the members of my body, waging war against the law of my mind and making me a prisoner of the law of sin at work within my members. What a wretched man I am! Who will rescue me from this body of death?"*

Father, I identify with Paul because I know that when I don't confront these conflicts in my emotions, I allow them to set up a barrier between us. You do not create this barrier. I create it! My punishment then is to be separated from you. I no longer have your peace and your power flowing through me. So, along with the Apostle Paul, I can also say, *"What a wretched man I am. Who will rescue me from this body of death?"*

Thanks be to God through Jesus Christ our Lord! Romans 7:25.

Therefore, now there is no condemnation for those who are in Christ Jesus. Romans 8:1

No condemnation! No condemnation! No condemnation!

Self-imposed separation, yes! Condemnation, no!

More than ever in this battle, Father, a battle which has been so fierce lately, I need to continually be reminded of your grace and forgiveness; that I need not, and should not, carry any guilt around; that I should not stoop down, I should not lower myself to pick up any guilt once is has been washed away by the blood of my Savior. To dwell on the guilt is to sin against you, by doubting your Word which tells me of your forgiveness. When I choose to carry a sense of guilt, this not only creates further sin, it maintains the barrier between us that blocks the flow of your peace and power into my life, into my "members" as the Apostle Paul puts it. There is nothing holy about that, nothing! For this kind of demeanor reflects defeat, and does nothing to reflect your glory through a forgiven life. How sad that is; how it must hurt you, Father, when I do this.

Just as this conflict, this battle within me, has been so fierce, so much deeper has come my appreciation of your grace. There is such freedom in this, and through this freedom comes victory – victory which brings glory, praise and honor to you. There is then no looking back; it is only to look ahead – going forward in the power of your Holy Spirit.

The greater the battle, the greater the victory!

Thank you, Father, for this gift on Father's Day, this gift of reminding this earthly father, self-imposed separation, yes; condemnation, no!

TRANSITIONS
Reflections of Blessing and Encouragement

Father, in reflecting back over this past week, and the meditations that you gave to me, I am in awe!

How often during this time I felt as if I didn't belong in your presence, beset with guilt and doubt. My prayers and my thoughts seemed to have no pattern to them. They seemed so empty! I think down deep I knew you were there, but I felt disconnected from you.

Yet, as I read my journal entries from this week, I see them from a truly different perspective. I am touched by your divine presence through the words you gave me. Once again you have revealed to me that you were there all the time, guiding my thoughts as I wrote, even though my feelings at the time told me otherwise.

Wow!! It was not an "empty" week, after all. How blessed and encouraged I am.

In the name of Jesus, I thank you and I praise you.

TRANSITIONS
Your Word – The Divine Dimension

These words from Psalm 132:3-5, touch my heart this morning, Father:

I will not enter my house or go to my bed – I will allow no sleep to my eyes, no slumber to my eyelids, till I find a place for the LORD, a dwelling for the mighty one of Jacob.

I will not begin my day, nor will I end my day; I will not sleep until I acknowledge you, O Lord, until I praise you and thank you, O Father God, until you are consciously in my thoughts, until I hold tightly to the Sword of your Spirit.

For therein lie all the riches that you intended for us to have. Therein lies your rhythm for today. Someone once described this rhythm to me as a "spiritual smorgasbord," which contains your peace, your strength, your power, your compassion, your love and your energy. And, also within this rhythm is that which I covet the most, your wisdom, and your divine discernment. If I choose to think on your Word, then it all comes to me.

Therein lies the divine, supernatural dimension to my life. This is the dimension which brings a life of adventure and not a life of drudgery as some would choose to think. This is the dimension that reflects glory, praise and honor to you.

Oh, what a wonderful mystery this all is.

TRANSITIONS
My Psalm of Praise and Thanksgiving

It's May 1st already. On this day, I offer you my psalm:

Father, here in the quiet stillness of this morning,
my heart turns to you.

I ask you for your forgiveness of my sinful heart;
I ask this in the name of Jesus, my Savior and my Lord.

I am mindful of how his blood was shed for me on that awful cross;
how his blood washes me, so that I can stand before you
forgiven, spotless and clean.

My gratitude to you, Lord Jesus,
is best shown by the man that I strive to be.

From my forgiven heart, I can praise you, Father;
you who are the omnipotent God of the universe;
over all things, the creator of the universe,
God of all Gods, the one true God.

I am continually uplifted by your faithful presence.
You are always with me.
The encouragement that this brings to me is immeasurable.

Your Word I carry in my heart;
It is my weapon to slash through all of the fears
and doubts the enemy lays before me.
It always brings victory – always!

With your Sword in my hand, I am always victorious;
I am never defeated.

My joy in you knows no bounds, Father;
for in Christ Jesus and the power of your Holy Spirit,
I have that joy always.
Always, the reflection of joy
brings glory, praise and honor to you.

Were it not for my quiet time with you, I would be lost;
the awesome mystery of your divine presence
is beyond my human understanding.
But within that mystery, your presence is so real,
so very, very real.

Father, may my praise to you;
may the man that I am in you bring you joy.
May our fellowship be rich to you
beyond my human understanding.

In the name of Jesus,
in and through the power of your Holy Spirit,
may my life always reflect glory, praise and honor to You.

Father, I offer this psalm to you this morning as thanksgiving for all that you give to me, for all that you mean to me, and to praise you as my Lord and my God

TRANSITIONS
An Intimate Relationship

6:45AM

Here I am, Father. The first thought on my mind when I awoke this morning, was spending time with you in your Word.

I know that lately I have not been as faithful about our morning quiet time together as I might be. Even when I am with you here, I have recently been struggling with the idea that I don't pray enough for others. I have been wondering if my prayers are too self-centered. And yet, I can honestly say (and you know the truth in my heart about this) that in these morning quiet times I do want to fellowship with you and get to know you better. This is exactly what I want! And it has happened over and over again through this journal, that you have revealed yourself to me over the years.

These revelations have enriched my life beyond my wildest expectations. Listening to you through these meditations brings me a deeper and more meaningful fellowship with you than if I were continually making prayer requests to you. Then, when I do make these requests, Father, I sense your listening presence, and I realize that it comes from the close relationship with you that has grown through these morning quiet times.

I could say, "First the relationship, then the requests and the petitions." For without a relationship, without knowing you, how else could I ever present my requests *"with thanksgiving"* (Philippians 4:6) and with the assurance that you do hear me?

Whether I am praying for myself or for others, in my heart I have absolute assurance of two things, Father. I know that you hear every prayer, every request, every petition. You hear every one of them. And, I know that you answer every one of them. Why would a loving God shrug off any of my prayers? Why would a loving God refuse to answer any request that I make to my Heavenly Father? My intimate relationship with you through my Lord Jesus gives me the freedom to ask for anything in his name.

You do hear, and you do answer. Your answer may not always be when or what I want it to be, but that is okay. The peace that I have in my heart knowing your answers are always for the best is reassurance enough.

I hear folks say, "I don't think God hears my prayers." I also hear them say, "God doesn't answer my prayers." I guess I can understand why these things are said, but it disappoints me every time I hear such comments. How it must disappoint you, Father, your Holy Spirit and you, Lord Jesus.

I am so thankful that your Word has come alive for me and for the joy I have in knowing the divine presence of the God who created the universe.

Wow!

Oh, what a wonderful mystery this all is!

TRANSITIONS

Knowing Your Will

Father, I hear folks say all the time, "I want to know God's will for my life."

So do I!

So, how do we find this out? We find this out through the simple expedient of communicating with you. I use the term "simple expedient" because much of the time we tend to make it more complicated than it really is.

Players do not know the coach's plan for the game they are going to play unless they listen to the coach. Players do not just walk out onto the field, onto the court, and have the coach's plan just drop on them from above. They have a playbook which they have to commit to memory in order to spontaneously put the plays into motion while playing the game. They don't have time to stop and think about every move, i.e., "What does the playbook say that I do now." No!

These plays must be so deeply ingrained in their minds that they can execute them without consciously thinking about what they are doing. This truth is so evident that it seems ridiculous to even mention it. And yet there seem to be many well-meaning Christians who want to know your will, Lord (or at least we think that we do), but we take no steps to find it out. Sitting in church on Sunday morning will rarely, I believe, fully reveal your will to anyone.

If I am going to be walking in your will all the time, then I have to be in constant communication with you, Father. The Apostle Paul gives us the same instructions when he tells us to *"pray continually"* (1 Thessalonians 5:17).

This all starts by learning the playbook, by spending quiet one-on-one time in your locker room, O Lord, reading and meditating on your Word. The more my heart is saturated with your Word, the more your Holy Spirit influences my thoughts and the stronger becomes my communication with you. This, I think, is "praying continually."

A team that shows up for practice only for one or two hours on Sunday morning is a team that will lose every game.

If we as Christians want to be victorious over the enemy, who is constantly trying to occupy more of the time on the playing field of our minds, then we constantly have to strengthen our game plan by dwelling on our playbook, your Word. Then, the concept of how to know your will, your good and perfect will for our lives, seems pretty simple, doesn't it? It is through the simple expedient of communicating with you.

The heroes of our faith all had one thing in common. They all devoted a portion of their daily schedule to spending quiet one-on-one time with you in your Word. What made them successful in doing this? They took the time to do it because they wanted to do it.

I am blessed to have experienced this. Although I all too often falter in maintaining that constant communication with you, I still know the "how" of seeking his *good, pleasing and perfect will.*" (Romans 12:2)

TRANSITIONS
My Heroes

Father, I want to thank you for two heroes in my walk of faith with you. Both of these men, Dr. Charles Stanley and Dr. Chuck Swindoll, have fed me with the riches and the reality of your Word. Both of them have deep insights into the Christian life that could only come from their spending a lot of one-on-one time with you. Both have used their speaking gifts to be able to communicate deep truths from you in ways that I can understand; in ways that I can relate to my own life.

Many brothers and sisters in our faith have their own heroes. Often these are their own pastors, for there are many pastors who are not well known, but who faithfully minister day in and day out to those within their own church families. Two of my own pastors who are included in my club of heroes are Pastor Garry Shirk and Pastor Jeff Raker.

I am grateful to all of these men for how they have inspired me to grow.

We all need these earthly heroes, Father. Keep your arms tightly around them so that they will always have the strength to handle whatever temptations may come their way, that their profiles will always honor you.

I once heard Dr. Charles Stanley say, "Don't you give me any credit." Well, Father, he is right. The glory here is yours. However, I can still thank him and all of my other heroes for having hearts that were open to your leading, and for their desire to continually venture into that canyon of one-on-one time with you in your Word.

Wow! I am amazed, Father, at how your glory reflects itself, not only in the lives of our heroes, but in all of us when we live the adventure of walking with you.

TRANSITIONS
Refocusing My Thoughts

Father, thoughts of all of the projects that I want to get done today at the office are fighting for control of my mind this morning. There is a definite tension, a pressure in this thought pattern that manifests itself by generating a mindset which makes me want to hurry to my desk so that I can get all these things done, so that when tomorrow comes I'll be completely caught up!" I can't believe that I allow myself to do this!

But, in the midst of this bombardment, you have led me to reflect back to a meditation in a journal from several years ago. The thoughts you gave to me on that morning are just as relevant to me today as they were then. They challenge me again to learn how to live in the now, instead of focusing on the next project or the next day. I am again reminded that I must continuously look to you for strength and help in this matter.

When I think on your Word, when I make a conscious choice to pull snippets of your Word from my memory bank, and then silently say them to myself, I am in awe of how your Holy Spirit feeds my thoughts, of how you speak to me in this way, how you listen to me, how you comfort me, how you encourage me. This communication is so wonderful, and yet, so unexplainable. It always slows me down so that I can refocus my thoughts back to your priorities.

I need not understand the "how" of it, for this is a supernatural thing that my mortal, human mind cannot comprehend. And yet, this communication, this fellowship with you, is so very, very real.

Oh, what a wonderful mystery this all is.

TRANSITIONS
Trying to Run on an Empty Tank

Father, here I go again! I confess that my mind is trying to run ahead of both of us this morning. I continue to allow my thoughts to dwell on all of the projects and assignments that await me on my voice mail. I want to hurry and get on with them. Is it because I am somewhat doubtful, even fearful, of being able to do them? Or is it that looming illusion of wanting to be caught up? Being "caught up" so that I can do *what?*

There is no energy, no fuel for my efforts whenever I run ahead of you. I know that! And yet, I still do it. Shame on me, especially since I know where to go to get the fuel for the energy to counteract these empty thoughts. All I have to do is to make the choice to drive up to the pump of your Word, and allow your Holy Spirit to fill my thoughts with it.

I am so grateful for your grace which allows me, through a forgiven heart, to return to the source of energy which always fills my tank.

TRANSITIONS
Stuck in Park

5AM

Father, I seem to be "stuck" in my thoughts this morning. They seem to be going nowhere.

I know of a number of things I can pray for, but I can't seem to shift the gears of my mind out of "park."

Here I am, up early enough that I have plenty of time; and yet, here I sit.

Well, at least I am honestly sharing my thoughts with you, and I still *know* that you are listening and that you hear me. Thank you for the reassurance of your presence.

Somehow, I have the peace of knowing that I will eventually shift into a "higher gear" today.

In the name of Jesus, I thank you, and I praise you.

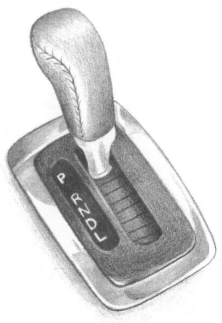

TRANSITIONS
Energy from Praise – Psalms 145-150

I love these "praise Psalms," Father. They are so special to me.

It never fails. I can be down in the dumps over something, or even nothing. I can be discouraged. I can be almost overwhelmed with some particular concern. There are numerous other mindsets with negative overtones that occasionally like to rear their ugly heads.

But, no matter what my situation or mindset is, when I start reading aloud beginning at Psalm 145, and continue on to 146, to 147, 148, 149 and conclude with 150, the transformation of my outlook which occurs on that short road in your Word is still baffling to me. I always come off of that short journey with a positive attitude. Always!

It's like driving my car through the car wash. I show up with a dirty car, and I drive it into the car wash. When I come out the other side, after a very short journey, my car is clean. All the dirt is gone. And, it's funny, but every time I am driving away from the car wash with a clean car, it seems like my car runs better. I'm sure that it doesn't, but it sure seems like it does. I can't really explain that phenomenon either.

Father, the energy that comes from praising you is somewhat of a mystery to me. I don't know how it works, but bringing praise to you always lifts my spirits. It always encourages me. Maybe it's because praising you reminds me of what a great God you are. Praising you seems to bring the vastness of your power and love into play. This somehow reminds me that you can do all things – all things! There is nothing that you cannot do. I find great comfort in this, Father.

Praising you creates a humble heart within me. This is always good. Praising you brings me a thankful heart. Praising you adds another dimension to the joy that I have in knowing you. Even now, I notice that my energy is being renewed as I write these words.

Sometimes I think we don't give enough emphasis to praising you in our Christian walk. Perhaps more needs to be said and shared about what can happen when we open to you the gates of praise in our hearts.

Oh, what a wonderful mystery this all is.

TRANSITIONS
Friendships Restored / Memories Renewed

Father, I never would have thought it possible. The renewed contact and closeness with some of the guys that I grew up with brings a dimension of warmth and richness to my life that I never imagined. The medium of email makes it possible for us to be in constant communication with each other, sharing "new" old memories every week.

Our dear friend, Jerry, who we affectionately called "Monk," recently went home to be with you. As much as he is missed, what has buoyed our spirits are all of the good memories we have of him. We loved to get on him about the time we were in Carter's Restaurant when he went to put salt on his hamburger, and the lid came off and dumped the whole shaker on it. One of the wiseacres in our crowd had purposely unscrewed it so that would happen. Monk didn't think it was as funny as we did. Memories like this mean a lot to all of us, helping us to overcome our sadness in losing him.

I thank you also, Father, for all the fun memories that we have of our dear friend, Dick. The guy we referred to as "The Barrel," kept us constantly uplifted. Just being around him always lifted my spirits. Every time he came around, when we hadn't seen him in awhile, we'd all break out in a chorus of that old song, "Roll Out the Barrel!" He has been home for two years now, and our memories of him are still vivid. Like Jerry, we will always remember him fondly.

The passing of Dick and Jerry have given the rest of us a much deeper appreciation for the friendships that we share. May we make the most of every opportunity we have to stay in touch in the years ahead. If there are other old friends whose spirits would be lifted by being a part of our old "gang," I pray that you would orchestrate their locating us. I know that such a thing is no problem for you, Father. Watching it happen would bring praise and glory to you.

May our memories remain full of those ball games, pranks and other fun things that we did growing up, and may our abilities always enable us to be able to dig deeply into that wonderful catalog of those happy times.

May we never lose the appreciation for our yearly reunions in Chicago. May the distances from Arizona, Florida and Cincinnati never deter us from getting together, and may we never miss out on any opportunity to laugh our insides out. I humbly thank you that our Chicago reunions have been belly laughs from the time we arrive until the time that we leave to go home. Wow!! What a blessing!! I pray that the health of each one will remain strong enough to enable us to continue to make that trip.

I love these guys, Father; Bob I., Bob D., Dave D., Jerry, Sam and Don! Thank you for this rich dimension in my life of friendships restored and memories renewed.

Postscript:

Father, I have to come back to this meditation to praise and glorify you because Don is going to join us for the first time on our trip to Chicago. Thank you for bringing him our way. May his time with his old friends be richer than he could ever imagine.

I thank you, and I praise you for all the little things that you do for us; the things we are all too often reluctant to ask of you.

TRANSITIONS
In the Storm

Father, I feel like a man wandering about in the wilderness; a ship adrift in the fog with no sense of direction, its rudder flapping uselessly, disconnected from its controls on the ship; a man out in the desert sandstorm, the grains of sand stinging my face.

My demons swirl all around me. They pull me in the wrong directions. They are constantly placing their evil temptations in my path, beckoning my thoughts and my actions into their lurid world. At times I almost feel powerless to stop them, even though I have the sword of your Spirit, your Word, in my hands and in my heart.

Yet, even in the midst of the storm I am blessed to know the truth of verse 105 of Psalm 119, "Your word is a lamp to my feet and a light to my path." When I turn to it, and I think on it, pulling it from my memory, it activates your Holy Spirit within my thoughts. It becomes my compass in the wilderness. It becomes the rudder to guide my ship through the fog. It becomes my oasis in the desert. It becomes the sword of your Spirit, my weapon to go on the offensive against my temptations.

Psalm 119 encourages me:

Your word, O LORD, is eternal; it stands firm in the heavens. (v 89)

If your law had not been my delight, I would have perished in my affliction. (v 92)

You are my refuge and my shield; I hope in your word. (v 114)

Save me for I am yours; I have sought out your precepts. (v 94)

I will never forget your precepts for by them you have preserved my life. (v 93)

Your statutes are my heritage forever; they are joy of my heart. (v 111)

There is now a new sense of direction. The fog lifts. The sandstorm stops. The advancement of my temptations is halted.

Once again, I experience a victory in this ongoing battle.

In the Name of Jesus, I thank you, and I praise you.

TRANSITIONS

Holiday Frustrations... and Joys

Father, I bring this to you because, as mundane and unimportant as it may seem, I feel that I need to lay this matter before you. You are a loving God who hears all of our prayers, even the so-called "little ones." All too often, our holidays bring a unique level of frustration; a combination of fatigue, apprehensiveness, and even that dreaded word, "worry!"

We wear ourselves out as we hurry to get everything done. The house has to be spit-shined, special food prepared, and all the right gifts purchased. We become apprehensive over whether everything will go smoothly and everyone will behave themselves and get along, and whether we can arrive on time wherever we are going. We worry about the whole scenario, anxious that everything will all turn out beautifully like a story on the "Hallmark Hall of Fame." It seems as if our holidays may well be one of the greatest casualties of our ninety-plus miles-per-hour lifestyle.

Father, I ask for your forgiveness for my part in all of this. Sometimes I feel so guilty about it. May I remember to be thankful for those holidays that do turn out to be joyous celebrations, for they provide opportunities to connect families together in a festive atmosphere. They bring laughter and create new memories. I thank you for the expectation and anticipation of the Christmas season, for the beautiful lights and decorations that go up at Thanksgiving and last into the New Year. Thank you for the memories of the birthday party that turned out to be a complete surprise. Thank you for the many holiday traditions that are foundational in providing joy in our culture.

Thank you, Father, for this joyful perspective that blots out all of those frustrations. Shame on me, I guess, for even allowing them to have any place in my mind.

TRANSITIONS
Suffering... and Joy!

Father, there is something I don't understand. I have heard a lot of preaching and many comments from my fellow believers about the suffering, the discipline and the sacrifice that we must go through as we follow our Lord and Savior, Jesus Christ.

I can understand our sharing in his suffering, but there is something that disturbs me about all of this emphasis on suffering and sacrifice. I hear very little about the joy that we have in our relationship with you through our Lord Jesus, about having the power *"to grasp how wide and long and high and deep is the love of Christ"*(Ephesians 3:18), and of our being *"able to do immeasurably more than all we ask or imagine, according to his power that is at work within us"* (Ephesians 3:20).

This is the same power, the same joy at work within us that caused the Apostle Paul to express, *"I consider everything a loss compared to the surpassing greatness of knowing Christ Jesus, my Lord"*(Philippians 3:8). He continues in verse 10 to say that he *"wanted to know Christ and the power of his resurrection and the fellowship of sharing in his suffering."*

This is the same power, your power at work within us, which enables us to grasp an understanding of the magnitude of your love and enables you to do more in us, *"than all we ask or imagine"*. If there is not joy in that, then there is not joy in anything. You have made the joy that is available to us very obvious in your Word. Even in the midst of whatever sufferings may come our way, the *joy* we experience in relationship with you is always there.

Your Word tells us in Romans 5:3-5, that *"we also rejoice in our sufferings because we know that suffering produces perseverance;*

perseverance, character; and character, hope. And hope does not disappoint us, because you, O God, have poured out your love into our hearts by your Holy Spirit, which you have given us."

This is a diorama of victory, not defeat! Why then, is the *joy* which is part of the equation almost never talked about whenever suffering is being extolled? Why? I do not understand! It seems as if we are afraid of the joy because we might somehow be disappointed. What kind of faith is that, really? How this must disappoint you, Father.

My old friend, Pastor Garry Shirk, used to lament the low self-esteem that we all too often have as believers. How many of us want to be around Christians who are "down in the mouth?" Rather, wouldn't we prefer to be around believers who reflect joyful hearts because of their relationship with you in Christ Jesus?

Father, I don't want to "pick up a cross and follow Jesus" just because some spiritually well-intentioned soul says that I have to. I don't want to just "suffer for suffering's sake." What a negative connotation this brings to our walk with Christ. No wonder so many people are turned off by the gospel message. After all, who really does want to "suffer?" I know that I sure don't!

But am I willing to pick up the cross because I *love*? Yes! Yes! Because of what you have done for me in Christ Jesus am I willing to be obedient to the point of suffering? Yes, I am willing because I love, and because of the joy I have in you; *not* because of a bunch of misunderstood church rules.

I remember a time when I let you down in my response to a particular situation, and then wept bitterly because I felt that I had hurt the Father who loved me so much. Recalling that situation still brings tears to my eyes. Though the memory of my failure is painful, I am glad to be reminded just how easy it is to allow circumstances to dictate my response. How could I ever have kicked aside the joy that I have in you? How could I *ever* hurt you like that?

To be willing to suffer for the *joy* set before me... *yes*! That is my desire, Father. May I always be strengthened by your joy!

TRANSITIONS
Silence

My silence, Father, ...so that I might *listen*.

Is the blankness of the preceding page just a little disturbing? Shouldn't there be something written there? Do we sometimes have trouble with "gaps" in a conversation, when no one is talking, and there is only silence?

Without *Silence,* can we really *listen?*

TRANSITIONS
Listening

Listening means *no words* from me, Father, rather, that I would listen to you in your Word, and be a listener to the words of others.

TRANSITIONS
Your Faithful Word

He sends his command to the earth. His word runs swiftly."
Psalm 147:15

Father, your Word is for everything, everywhere.

Its power has no limit.

It binds me to you; it quickens your Holy Spirit within me, within my thoughts.

It encourages me. It reminds me of how faithful and loving you are.

It restores my joy, the deep, indescribable joy that I have through my relationship with you.

It never ever fails me, Father. Never! For you never fail me.

Oh, what a blessing to know you through knowing your Word.

May my life always reflect all that you are in me through your Word, in a way that brings glory, praise and honor to you.

TRANSITIONS
Joy in Obedience

Father, it grieves my heart when I hear preaching and teaching which implies that obedience to you involves only drudgery, pain, trials and tribulations. True, these things are, at times, a part of our being obedient to you.

As with suffering, we far too often seem to be afraid to speak of the joy which comes from our obedience. *"And we pray this in order that you may live a life worthy of the Lord and may please him in every way: bearing fruit in every good work, growing in the knowledge of God, being strengthened with all power according to his glorious might so that you may have great endurance and patience, and joyfully giving thanks to the Father"* (Colossians 1:10-12).

Are we afraid of watering down the meaning of obedience when we emphasize how it brings joy? Certainly, a joyful life is the best witness for you, Lord, for it reflects a life of victory which encourages others.

On the other hand, allowing the drudgery of legalism to be the hallmark of our Christian character does nothing to further your Kingdom. All this does is run people away from you, Father. This type of countenance reveals anything but a joyful and victorious life!

Oh, that the true message revealed by your Word would permeate our Christian community! Help us to grasp the truth that obedience to you means knowing your constant presence in a way that brings all of the fruits of your Holy Spirit to bear in our lives, and the joy of total victory.

TRANSITIONS
On Having Doubts
Be Quiet, Listen and Move On!

How often I have to remind myself that doubting something does not mean that these doubts will be fulfilled. I can choose to challenge my doubts, to forge ahead into the midst of them and to move through them.

I need to just be quiet, listen and move on! Unnecessary words, whether spoken or unspoken, only expend energy that could be used in more constructive ways. If those words are a reflection of negative thoughts, then they can have even more of a draining effect on our energy. Quieting our spirits prevents this waste of energy and lays the foundation for thought patterns that can overcome the doubts.

Any of us can use a thought displacement technique in this situation simply by finding something positive to think about. But there is a far better, more long-lasting approach to use here, and that is to recall scripture from our memory bank. Of course, it has to be there in the first place, which means that some verses have to be committed to memory. Once imbedded in our hard drive, God's Word can be pulled up onto the monitor of our thoughts, allowing the Holy Spirit to infuse his supernatural power into our minds. This not only changes our thought patterns at that moment, but it continues to develop in us a whole new mindset, as if to build a wall against the confusion which results from our doubts.

The result can be a *changed life,* where our minds become a strong fortress against doubt. We need a fortress, because there is a battle going on. Like soldiers who never leave the ramparts, we must always be armed and on guard against attacks from the enemy who is relentless in his desire to weaken and destroy; an enemy who seeks to undermine our faith with doubt.

When we are armed with the Word, the Holy Spirit gives us the power to use this sword against the enemy (Ephesians 6:17). It is not our own power which provides the momentum for the sword, it is his power. The swing of the sword becomes so strong that is slashes through the enemy, cutting down his forces – our doubts – one by one as they surge against us.

I like Hollywood imagery here, where a vast army of evil demons and goblins is charging into the ranks of the good guys. In the battle that follows, the bad guys are cut down by the swords of the good guys. And then the enemy retreats, but he is not totally destroyed. He will attack again as soon as he observes that we have put down our swords.

TRANSITIONS
Horizons

Father, at this time in my life, there are many new horizons before me. Just like pieces in a puzzle, I wonder where they will all fit. When I think about it I realize that I don't need to know how they will all come together. I need only to go at each one, on faith, and then let you arrange all the pieces together into your pattern. Moving forward is up to me. Fitting it all together is up to you.

I am blessed to know that moving ahead on faith and trusting in you to guide me is the ultimate adventure in this life. Nothing compares with it. But my excitement and my emotions still cause me to run ahead of you and try to figure it all out by myself, even though I know better. This overcomes the peace I have in my heart that I always have when I wait upon you. I am like a little kid who runs down the road ahead of his dad rather than holding onto his hand as they journey together. This never works!

I don't know how these horizons will manifest themselves in my life. As I step back and look at them I see so many parallels between now and 1987 when we started our Agency. But, what is different now is that I have the experience of that era to reflect on. I draw strength from reflecting on that time of transition, for I realize that I now have a *knowing* of you that I did not have at that time. The engine of my faith is bigger and stronger than it was back then. Fueled by those experiences my engine now has components which enable me to fly at a higher altitude than ever before. Its power and efficiency are no longer hampered by the fear that formerly inhibited my ability to take flight.

Oh, that I would have the courage to go full throttle on this new engine and fly it to its maximum! Father, I ask that your Word would always serve as my instrument panel and your truth my compass on the adventure into new horizons.

The higher the flight, the brighter the glory to you!

TRANSITIONS
Faith and the Unknown

We walk with faith into each new phase of life, building on the wisdom of experience, but still welcoming the unknown that lies ahead in the next phase. Without the unknown there is no place for faith in you, Father God. This is the faith that enables you to show us the way, so that we can see your hand at work and grow in our knowing of you. This is the real adventure in living, an adventure that never has to end.

It only ends when we try to convince ourselves how *set* everything is, how everything is going to *be,* and when we think we know exactly what we are going to be *doing.* It happens when we choose to park our ship at the dock, to put our life into a box, into a structure.

Little by little emptiness becomes the result when we no longer welcome the adventure of the *unknown* into the next phase of life.

Father, your Word clearly shows us that we need not be afraid of the *unknown* and what it might hold for us. We are never alone; you make that perfectly clear throughout Scripture. We need only to pursue your objective, your will, into that *unknown.* The real adventure of knowing you more deeply makes our life fulfilling through every phase of life until you call us to the end of this earthly existence, and into the ultimate adventure of living forever with you.

TRANSITIONS
The Road Ahead

Father, how easy it is, how tempting it is, to want the road ahead to be smoothly paved, with every stop, every destination clearly marked out before us. How tempting to want to know that there will be no bends beyond very gentle curves and to know that there will be no ruts or potholes; that there will be no serious bumps along the way. How tempting it is to wish that there will be no bridges out which cause us to have to take detours. How tempting it is to want there to be no construction areas which slow us down. How tempting it is to want to know that there will be no forks which cause us any anguish over which road to take.

Father, help me never to be judgmental of those who appear to have made a bad choice in the road they have taken. May I only be concerned with the road that you have called me to take.

May I never need to be reminded that my walk of faith is an ongoing journey. It is never a *destination*.

May I always remember that you never send us out alone, Father. You are always faithful to be with us.

I ask that I will always be thankful for the courage and wisdom that you give me for the journey; thankful for the awesome privilege of being able to experience the ultimate adventure of walking the road that you have laid out for me. At those times when I begin to flinch, to weaken, to tire, show me how to rest in you; that I would not falter in fulfilling your purpose and your will for my life.

May I be ever mindful of your power that is at work with every step I take. And for the indescribable joy that the road ahead will bring, may I always be thankful.

May my journey bring glory, praise and honor to you.

TRANSITIONS

PART IV
Transitions Revisited

TRANSITIONS
Some Personal Reflections

In looking back, I can see why the Lord wanted me to make that move into my own Agency. It had nothing to do with money or lifestyle. It had everything to do with my becoming totally dependent upon him for the first time in my life.

In so doing, I have had the opportunity to keep a journal of the joyous journey that it has turned out to be, and to get a glimpse of the ultimate adventure of living a life that is totally dependent upon him. It is just a "glimpse," because all too often I find myself stepping off the path that God has for my life and going my own way.

I have discovered along this journey that there is a recurring pattern in my efforts to stay on God's path. First, I become overwhelmed when trying to do everything in my own limited strength and wisdom. This eventually ends up in frustration, confusion and concern that borders on fear. Then I am drawn back to spending quiet one-on-one time with him in the Word. This always results in getting to know him in a deeper way. Finally, I return to that "ultimate adventure," of being back on the path that he has set for me.

This book began with my reflections on the years from 1985-1989 when the intensity of a time of transition in my life was at its peak. Ironically, at the end of this journey through reflections and meditations of the past, I find myself at another turning point; another time of transition which involves moving out of my career as an insurance agent and into a new venture as a writer.

I wonder now as I did then, "Is this venture really going to go anywhere?" My doubts keep saying to me, "Really, John! You, a published author? C'mon, get real!" I can almost hear the chuckles of someone in the literary field who happens to stumble upon this book. Shame on me for having such doubts given the experience of my earlier transition. But, this time I know that my doubt is not in the Lord's faithfulness in guiding me. Rather, my doubt is in me. Will I be disciplined enough to keep my thoughts focused on him?

Will I be disciplined enough to spend quiet one-on-one time with him in the Word? I am blessed to know that that is the key for me. One would think, given the richness that has come from our fellowship over the years, that I would hurry to get there every morning!

My desire to add writing to my current insurance career assures me that I have not parked the ship of my life at the dock! I seem once again to be sailing around Cape Horn, with the winds of uncertainty blowing my ship backward, then forward, then sideways. But despite being tossed all over the place I continue to trust God as I sail ahead into unknown waters.

Cape Horn is at the southern tip of South America. With the wind currents converging there from both the Atlantic and Pacific Oceans, it is an area of constantly stormy seas. Sailing ships have always had a particularly difficult time making their way around the Horn. I have seen photos of such ships that had most of their masts blown completely off during the journey. Of course, this makes navigation rather difficult!

I now realize that there is a strong connection between this current transition period and the one of almost 25 years ago. Despite my self-doubt, and knowing that I might well get my masts blown off during this journey, my previous experience has taught me not to fear this new time of transition, but rather to welcome the adventure in it. The result has become the discovery of a whole new realm of creative thinking. And, thinking creatively is fun!

How sad it is when we no longer welcome change into our lives, for these changes can produce the greatest opportunities for our faith to be put into action. Faith requires trust; trust in the Lord that he will guide our ship as it sails through turbulent waters like those of Cape Horn.

We all have "Cape Horns" as part of the transitions in our lives. But when we refuse to sail through their stormy channels, we forfeit the adventure of putting our faith into action, trusting the wind of God's Holy Spirit to power us forward and to guide us.

And then, think about this; without that trust in him, we rob him of a chance to be glorified.

It is my heartfelt wish that you will keep on sailing, with your eye always on the lighthouse of God's Word!

TRANSITIONS
The Wavertree

Many times I have walked into homes or buildings, and there on
the wall in a very obvious setting, I have noticed a portrait of a tall,
square-masted sailing ship pushing forward under full sail. Perhaps this
image is so popular because it seems to represent the triumph of the
human spirit.

The Wavertree is a four-masted, square-rigged windjammer.
The windjammers were the descendents of the graceful wooden clipper
ships that preceded them in maritime history. Iron-hulled and twice as
large as the clippers, they were magnificent in appearance.

Majestic in her day, as with all windjammer ships when under
full sail, the Wavertree sailed the seven seas for almost twenty-five years
until the year 1910. During that year her journey around Cape Horn
proved to be the Waterloo of her sailing days. She became drawn into
the winds and high seas of a violent storm off of the Horn and lost most
of her masts. Her crew miraculously managed to keep her afloat until
she could drift to the safety of the Falkland Islands.

Lying forlornly at anchor in Port Stanley in the Falklands, her
decks littered with storm wreckage, this once magnificent ship was now
reduced to a dark and ugly hulk. No longer majestic under full sail, she
languished in maritime obscurity serving as a sand barge and floating
warehouse for the next five decades.

Then, in 1968, the Wavertree was brought to New York City by
the South Street Seaport Museum where she was restored to her former
glory. She was designated a national landmark in 1978. Visited and
admired by thousands every year, she proudly stands there today, the
largest iron sailing vessel still afloat.

The story of the Wavertree seems to be a fitting analogy in thinking about the transitions in our lives. Sometimes the winds of those transitions are calm. At other times, they seem to come at us from all directions. At those times it seems as if the pressures we face will surely cause the masts that hold the sails of our lives to break and come crashing down around us.

Yet no matter how strong the winds, no matter how bad the damage we sustain, through God's loving grace we can be restored to that ultimate Journey of Joy of accomplishing his purpose, bringing glory, praise and honor to him.

TRANSITIONS
Conclusion

I firmly believe that all God wants from us is for us to take some time out from our busy world, to *make* some time, to give him an opportunity to talk with us one on one.

PSALM 5:3

Morning by morning, O LORD,
you hear my voice;
morning by morning,
I lay my requests before you
and wait in expectation."

TRANSITIONS
Transitions Revisited – A Sequel?

Is there a period of transition in your life that you think would be helpful to share with someone? Perhaps there is someone totally unknown to you who would benefit from hearing about how God guided you through some stormy seas, those periods of rough waters involving relationships, overcoming the hurt of a betrayal, financial pressures, job and career changes.

Or, how about those positive transitions? Achieving a goal that is the fulfillment of a life-long dream? The expectations for the future from a young lady who is planning her wedding?

We learn so much from the experiences of others. Many times, it takes the lonliness out of our own journey. How comforting and encouraging it can be when we know that others have faced transitional periods in their lives that mirror our own.

We can only have the opportunity to identify with those experiences when others are willing to share them with us.

So, my friend, if you have a transition to share, please let me hear your story.

If we receive enough of those stories that are soothing to the soul, our plan is to publish them as a sequel to *"Transitions~A Journey of Joy."*

Mailing addresses are shown on the Contact Information page for both email and snail mail. Your story can be sent accordingly by whichever medium is most comfortable to you.

If God has used my transitional story to encourage others, then why would he not use yours as well?

Think about it, my friend!

Contact Information

If you have comments to share with the author or if you would like to share your own transitional experience, John Dodsworth can be reached via the contact information below:

Email — transitionsajourneyofjoy@gmail.com

Mailing address — P. O. Box 18670, Fairfield, OH 45018

Website — www.johncdodsworth.com

John is also available for speaking engagements. Feel free to contact him directly regarding his availability.

15537988R00077

Made in the USA
Charleston, SC
08 November 2012